I Forgive You For Your Diaper

Written by
A. Parent
(at 3 AM)

Copyright © 2024

All Rights Reserved.

Illustrations by Ekaterina Mironova

No part of this book may be reproduced in any form or by any electronic or mechanical means, including information storage and retrieval systems, without written permission from the author, except for the use of brief quotations in a book review.

forgivethediaper@gmail.com

ISBN: 979-8-9908429-2-2 (Paperback)
979-8-9908429-1-5 (Ebook)

To my sweet little, poop factory
(that seems to run 24 hours a day with no days off – clearly it's non-unionized)

I'll never forget the day I met you,
all soft and round and new.

Overwhelmed with love,
I couldn't guess the things you'd do.

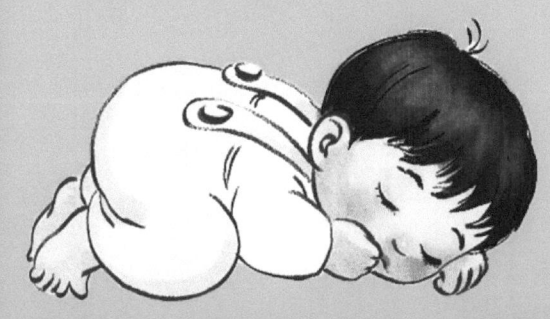

I swaddled you, coddled you,
only good things went in your tiny mouth.

But bad seemed to happen to all that good
on its journey south.

What went in as milk or pear or sometimes even guava,
burst out the exit door as stinking, glowing lava.

It happened all hours of day or night,
even Christmas morning.

In the car, stroller, bath, my arms,
the only constant was no warning.

I'd see your cheeks go red, and I'd fill with dread.
I knew that little focused face
foretold incoming toxic waste.

Before, you were hugged and kissed by family
and many other fans.

After, they'd sniff the air, become scared,
and remember other plans.

Your fog of doom would clear the room,
me alone as clean-up team.

I'll steel my nerves, chilled to the bone,
and face each new crime scene.

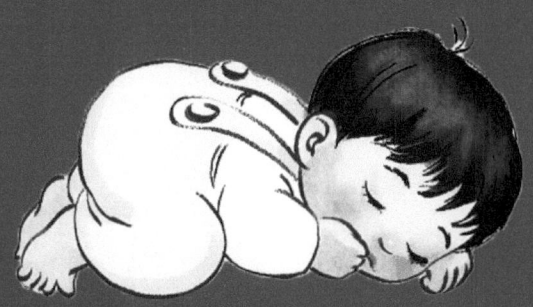

Stomach turning, my eyes burning,
I'd wonder how something so small and cute
could force me to put on a hazmat suit.

I'd add a welder's helmet, with a windshield wiper.
Then with a prayer, as if on a dare,
I'd approach your befouled diaper.

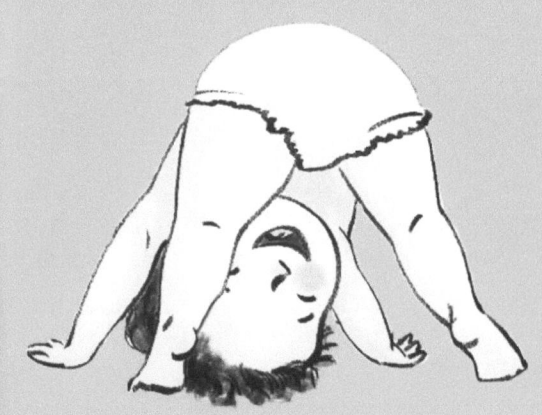

I'd change you, clean you, clean me, change me,
then grateful say "amen."

And then you'd scrunch your tiny nose, and do it all again.

Through nights and days and unrelenting weeks,
I'd ask "Why me? Why am I cursed with
this endless sewage leak?"

Yes, I grew upset, and was even getting bitter.

I felt bad for me, and double for the poor men
who came to collect our litter.

But those bad feelings left every time you'd smile,
my precious little mouse.

I forgot even those historic diapers,
where I thought I'd have to sell the house.

I know my love for you is stronger than any reeking stream of goo.

You're my child, my baby, and there's no task I wouldn't do.

So I forgive you for your diaper, and the smells that hide inside you.

(And just to be safe, I called your doctor, who confirmed nothing died inside you).

You're mine my dear, a wonderful little blessing.

A gift, a treasure, so of course
I forgive your frequent messings.

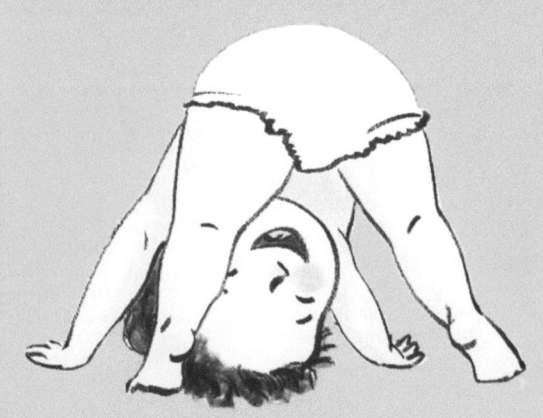

Dirty diapers are just you growing,
and everything will be fine.

Also, I take comfort knowing diaper revenge is coming,
because one day, you might be changing mine.

www.ingramcontent.com/pod-product-compliance
Lightning Source LLC
LaVergne TN
LVHW070441070526
838199LV00036B/678